Do We Yell in Class?

Seed
Learning

Do we yell
in class?

No, we don't.

We don't yell
in class.

Do we fight in class?

No, we don't.

We don't fight
in class.

Do we use phones in class?

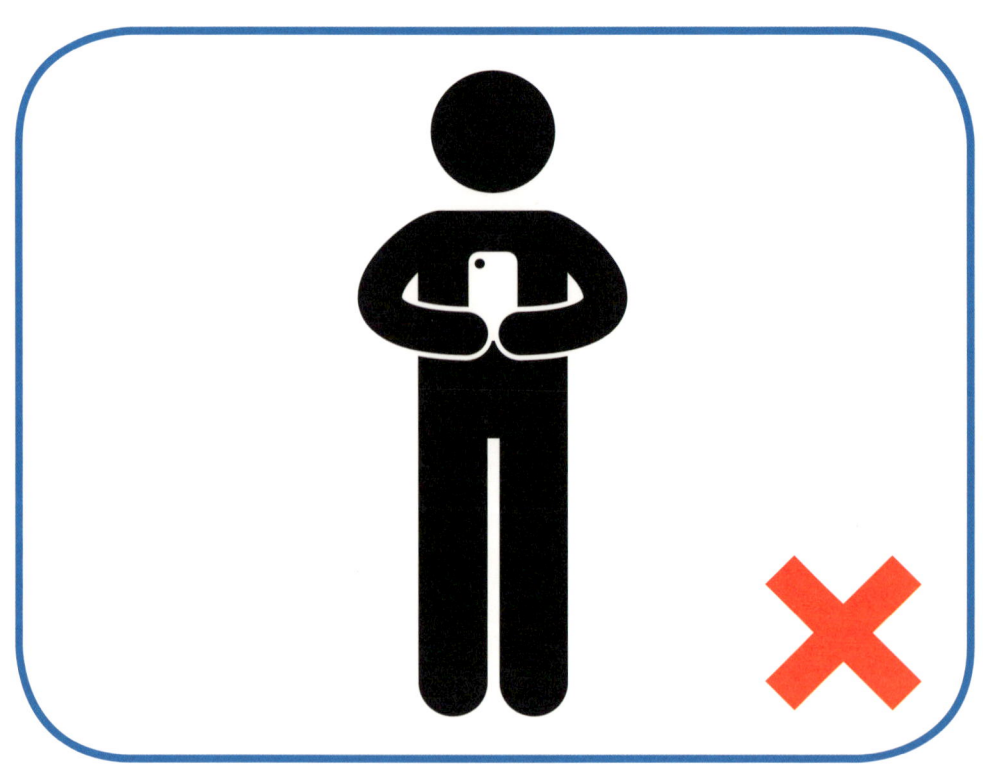

No, we don't.

We don't use phones
in class.

Do we run in class?

No, we don't.

We don't run in class.

Do we raise hands in class?

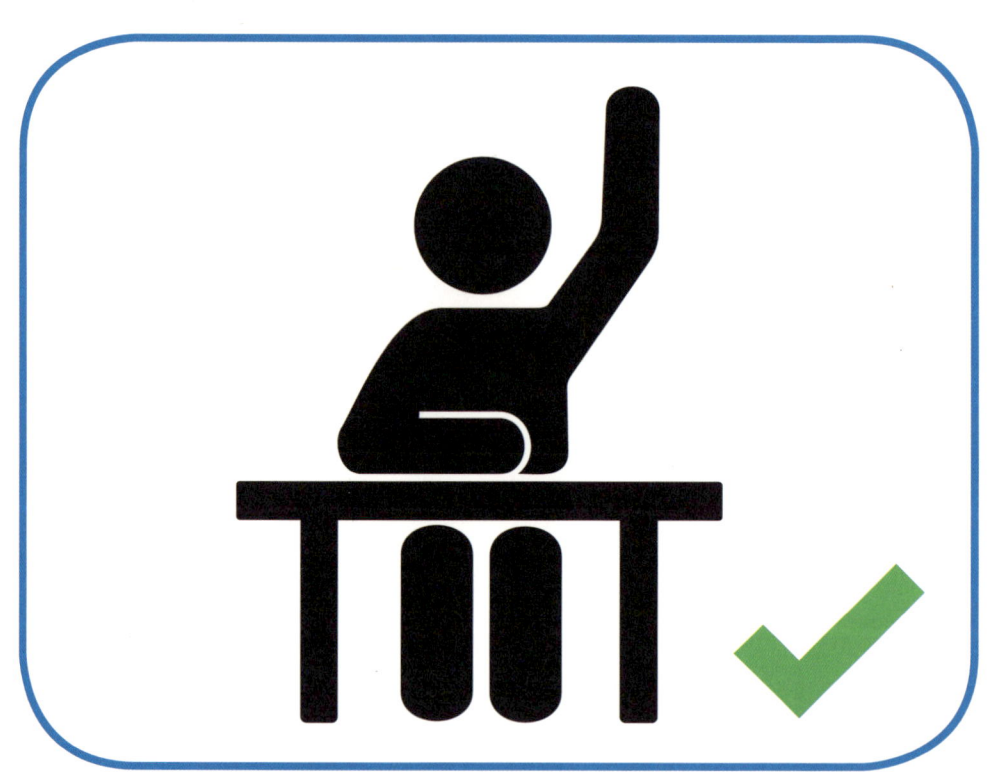

Yes, we do.

We raise hands
in class.

Do we share in class?

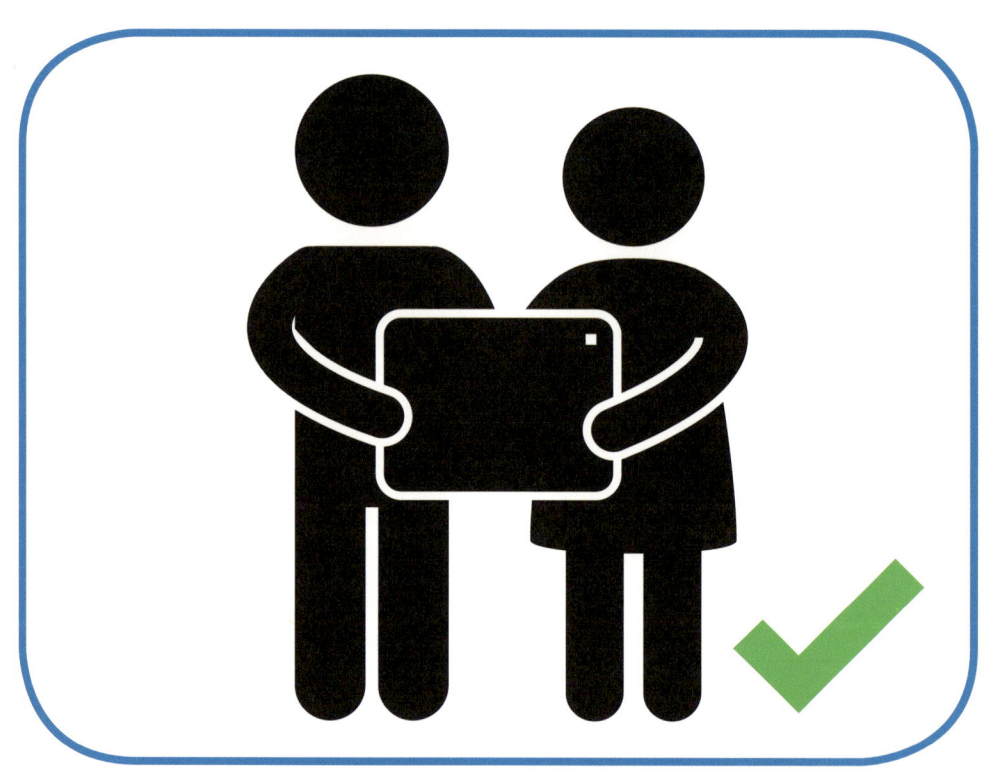

Yes, we do.

We share in class.

Do we listen in class?

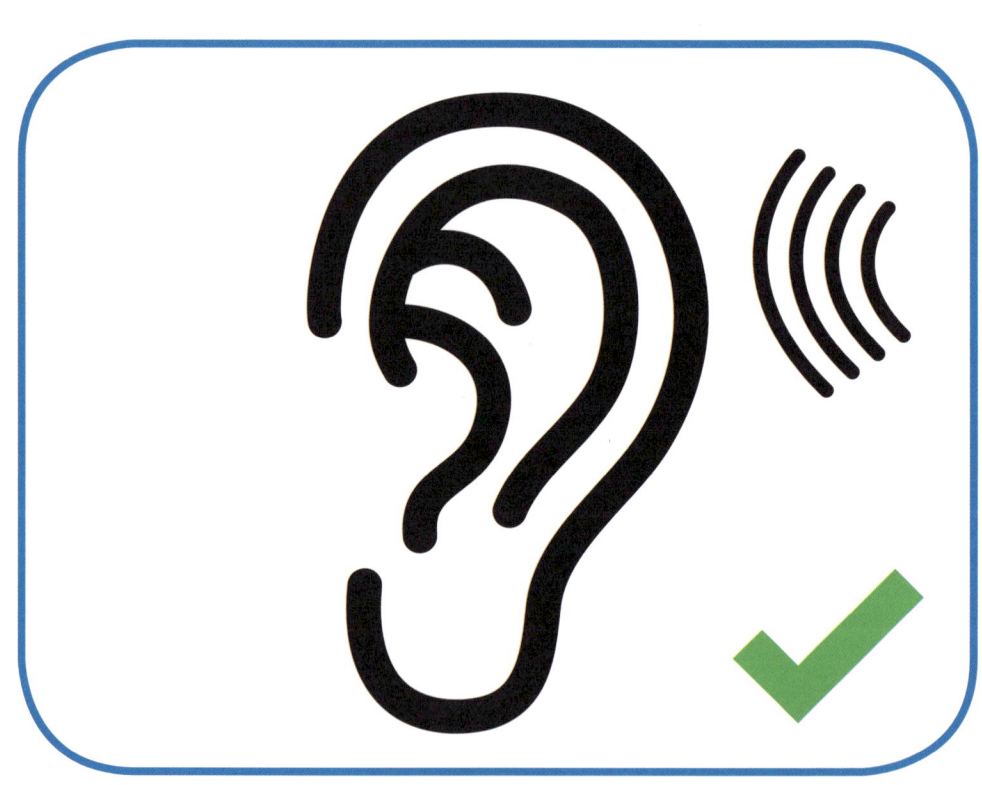

Yes, we do.

We listen in class.

Let's learn more about Valentine's Day.

Color the heart.